EXTREME JOBS IN EXTREME

LIFE ON AN
AIRCRAFT CARRIER

By Heather Moore Niver

Gareth Stevens
Publishing

Please visit our website, www.garethstevens.com. For a free color catalog of all our high-quality books, call toll free 1-800-542-2595 or fax 1-877-542-2596.

In memory of my grandfather, Keith Lowery, Aviation Machinist's Mate on the *USS Lexington CV-16*, and with tremendous thanks to Commander Daniel Packer

Library of Congress Cataloging-in-Publication Data

Niver, Heather Moore.
  Life on an aircraft carrier / Heather Moore Niver.
     p. cm. — (Extreme jobs in extreme places)
  Includes index.
  ISBN 978-1-4339-8493-8 (pbk.)
  ISBN 978-1-4339-8494-5 (6-pack)
  ISBN 978-1-4339-8492-1 (library binding)
  1. Aircraft carriers—Juvenile literature. I. Title.
  V874.N56 2013
  359.9'435—dc23
                                    2012022954

First Edition

Published in 2013 by
Gareth Stevens Publishing
111 East 14th Street, Suite 349
New York, NY 10003

Copyright © 2013 Gareth Stevens Publishing

Designer: Andrea Davison-Bartolotta
Editor: Therese M. Shea

Photo credits: Cover, p. 1 David A. Cox/U.S. Navy via Getty Images; courtesy of the U.S. Navy: p. 5 Mass Communication Specialist 2nd Class Julia A. Casper, p. 6 Mass Communication Specialist 3rd Class Zachary S. Welch, p. 9 Mass Communication Specialist Seaman Harry Andrew D. Gordon, p. 10 Chief Mass Communication Specialist Shawn P. Eklund, p. 11 U.S. Navy graphic, p. 14 Chief Photographer's Mate Dennis Taylor, p. 15 Mass Communication Specialist 1st Class Steve Smith, p. 17 Photographer's Mate 3rd Class Milosz Reterski, p. 18 Mass Communication Specialist Seaman William Cousins, p. 19 Mass Communication Specialist 1st Class Rachel McMarr, p. 20 Mass Communication Specialist 2nd Class Tony D. Curtis, p. 21 Mass Communication Specialist 3rd Class Tim D. Godbee, p. 23 Mass Communication Specialist 2nd Class Eric Crosby, p. 24 Photographer's Mate 3rd Class Joshua Karsten, p. 25 Photographer's Mate 1st Class Michael W. Pendergrass, p. 26 Mass Communication Specialist 3rd Class Deven B. King, p. 27 Photographer's Mate Airman Robert Brooks, p. 28 Mass Communication Specialist 3rd Class Joshua Scott, p. 29 Mass Communication Specialist 3rd Class Tiger Martinez; p. 7 Derek Gordon/Shutterstock.com; pp. 8, 13 Thomas J. Abercrombie/National Geographic/Getty Images; p. 16 Junko Kimura/Getty Images; p. 22 Damian P. Gadal/Shutterstock.com.

Printed in the United States of America

CPSIA compliance information: Batch #CS13GS: For further information contact Gareth Stevens, New York, New York at 1-800-542-2595.

CONTENTS

Words in the glossary appear in **bold** type the first time they are used in the text.

A CITY ON WATER

Aircraft carriers, also simply called carriers, carry airplanes and other aircraft. They're also floating airfields. Carriers are the "backbone" of the US Navy. They transport thousands of soldiers and everything they need to travel on the ocean for months. Because of this, carriers are sometimes called "cities on the sea."

Since carriers transport **weapons**, almost any job on board is dangerous. Planes launch and land on a carrier's deck at very high speeds. These aircraft carry bombs and **missiles**, so a small mistake can mean a big explosion. The pilots and crew on a carrier live with danger all day every day, even in times of peace.

KEEPING HEALTHY AT SEA

Even sailors need dental and medical checkups. The USS *Nimitz* aircraft carrier has five dentists. Six medical doctors are also available. The hospital has 53 beds. There's even a barbershop on board. The workers there give more than 1,500 haircuts each week!

Navies all over the world use aircraft carriers during war. In 1942, at the Battle of Midway, the United States changed the course of World War II when they sank four Japanese carriers.

A QUICK LOOK

The main body of a ship that floats in the water is called the hull. The flat area at the top of the carrier is called the flight deck. This is where aircraft take off and land. The island is a building on top of the flight deck. From here, officers watch what's going on and direct the crew.

Lots of action goes on below deck, too. A power plant creates electricity, and a **propulsion** system moves the carrier. Aircraft are stored in a large, covered space called a hangar. Also on the lower decks are living areas where sailors eat, sleep, and relax when they're off duty.

CHOW TIME

With more than 5,000 people on board, a carrier's kitchen staff has a hungry crew to feed. They might serve as many as 18,000 meals in a single day. That can mean grilling up more than 4,000 hamburgers, thousands of eggs, and stacks and stacks of pancakes every day.

Most of today's aircraft carriers have the same basic parts to make each carrier a powerful ship, an air force base, and a floating city all in one.

island

flight deck

hull

hangar

propulsion system

7

SERIOUS SHIPS

The US Navy uses three classes of aircraft carriers: Enterprise, Nimitz, and Ford. The Enterprise ships each have eight **nuclear reactors**. Enterprise was the first class of carrier powered by nuclear energy. These carriers are 1,040 feet (317 m) long and hold about 80 aircraft. They travel through the water at speeds of more than 30 **knots**, which is 35 miles (56 km) per hour.

Nimitz carriers are the largest class. They're 24 stories, or 244 feet (74 m) high, and can carry more than 5,000 sailors. The flight deck is 1,092 feet (333 m) long. That's longer than three football fields.

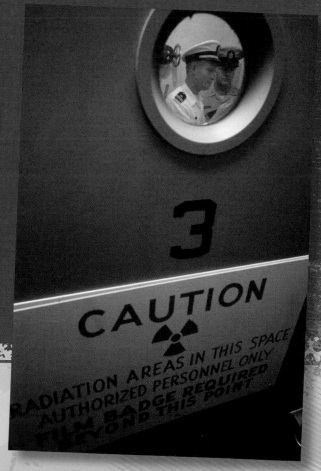

engine room door ▶

NUCLEAR-POWERED CARRIERS

Nuclear-powered carriers can sail for 15 to 20 years before they need to fuel! However, it can take several years to refuel a ship. Although they're long lasting, nuclear reactors are dangerous. They need protection and must be watched constantly to avoid a nuclear accident at sea.

Sailors working below deck near the reactor on the USS Enterprise only work shifts of 45 minutes at a time because temperatures can reach 140°F (60°C).

9

Like the Enterprise class, Nimitz carriers are nuclear powered. However, each Nimitz needs only two nuclear reactors. These supply plenty of power and allow more space for storage. The Nimitz ships can carry 50 percent more **ammunition** than most carriers and almost double the amount of aircraft fuel.

The newest class of carrier is the Ford, which is expected to set sail in 2015. Ford carriers will have two nuclear reactors, just like the Nimitz. They'll be 1,092 feet (about 333 m) long and reach speeds of more than 30 knots, or 35 miles (56 km) per hour.

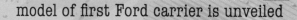
model of first Ford carrier is unveiled

FIERCE FORDS

Ford carriers will be able to hold 4,660 sailors and more than 75 aircraft. So far, Ford ships include PCU *Gerald R. Ford* and PCU *John F. Kennedy* ("PCU" stands for "Pre-Commissioning Unit," which means the ship isn't in use yet.) The Ford class will be the first carriers to have their lights and other services powered with electricity instead of steam.

CLOSE QUARTERS

It might seem cool to have a job sailing around the world and seeing new countries and people. Much of the time, however, crewmembers of a carrier don't see much besides the boat. Some sailors who work below deck might not see the sky for weeks at a time!

Most don't get the great views from the flight deck. This part of the ship has planes flying in and out, making it much too hectic and dangerous to allow extra people to walk around. Though the top of the island is safer, it's just a small space.

SWEET DREAMS

Berthing compartments are the areas where the sailors sleep. Beds, or racks, are lined up in stacks of three. Each crewmember has only a small storage bin and a locker for their things. Everyone in the compartment shares a bathroom, a common area, and one television.

Berthing compartments hold up to 60 crewmembers. Officers sometimes have a little more space and privacy, but not much.

AIRCRAFT STARTING & COOLING AIR

CONST STEAM

ALL COLORS ON DECK

With so much dangerous activity happening on the carrier's flight deck, sailors have to really focus on their jobs. Not a moment can be spared. To make everyone's role easy to recognize, each sailor on this deck wears a colored shirt, or jersey, to indicate their role. If there's ever a problem on a carrier, the color-coded shirts make it easy to spot someone who can help.

Sailors wear helmets with different colors to give more details about their job. Helmets may match the shade of their shirt or include additional colors. Crew in training wear yellow helmets bearing the letters "UI," which mean "under instruction."

ANCHORS AWAY

Working with anchors might not seem extreme, but it is if the anchor weighs 30 tons (27 mt)! A carrier's anchor is attached to a chain about 87 feet (27 m) long, with each chain link weighing about 400 pounds (182 kg). Heavy-duty motors move the anchors. Sailors stay out of the way so they won't be crushed.

anchor of USS *Theodore Roosevelt*

Sailors gather in the hangar of the USS Enterprise.

PILOTS

Pilots wear green or tan flight suits, different from the flight deck jerseys. They might have the most extreme carrier job. To take off, a plane needs to gain a lot of speed in a short distance. A machine called a catapult uses steam pressure to launch aircraft into the air. A jet can go from 0 to 165 miles (265 km) per hour in just seconds this way.

Landing on a carrier is even more dangerous. To keep from rolling off the runway, a tailhook is located at the back of the plane. The pilot lands so the hook snags a wire, called the arresting wire, which stops the speeding plane.

BROWN SHIRTS

Plane captains are crewmembers in brown shirts. When a pilot isn't in an aircraft, a plane captain is taking care of it. They check fluid levels, prepare it for flight, and make sure it's always ready for a mission. Plane captains spend 12 to 15 hours per day with their aircraft.

The runway is 500 feet (152 m) long. Some pilots describe their job as "landing on a postage stamp in the middle of the ocean"!

There are four sets of arresting wires on the flight deck. The first set is dangerously close to the edge of the deck. Snagging the second set is acceptable, but pilots usually aim for the third. The pilot has to figure out how to angle the aircraft to land exactly right.

Landing-signal officers (in white shirts) use radio commands and a system of lights to guide the pilot. If the pilot sees a yellowish-brown light in line with green lights, the plane is on target. When the plane hits the deck, the pilot **accelerates** because the plane needs power to take off if it doesn't catch the arresting wires.

TRICK OR TREAT

"Trick or treat" means a plane has such low fuel that the pilot has one chance to land on the carrier before the plane has to be refueled in midair. In the air, a fuel plane sends out a hose to connect the planes. It's a tricky process!

four sets of arresting wires

It's so hard to fuel a plane in the air that pilots say it's like driving on the freeway while trying to put a key in another car's trunk!

ANG

19

YELLOW SHIRTS

Engines roar and blades spin as planes, jets, and helicopters prepare to take off from the flight deck runway. Catapult and plane-handling officers in yellow shirts are on their guard every second. The deck is so loud crewmembers can't hear each other speak. Yellow shirts direct pilots and crew with arm and body signals.

Many signals are used on the deck. For example, to show that it's not clear for aircraft to take off, a handling officer holds out a hand just below the waist and gives a "thumbs down" sign. At night, yellow wands with lights make movements more visible.

SEA OF GREEN

In general, bright green shirts are the most common sight on an aircraft carrier deck. Green shirts have a variety of jobs. They check the catapults and arresting wires. They hook the plane to the catapult before takeoff. Some provide landing signals for helicopters.

When the crew is at its busiest, planes can land or take off from the deck every 25 seconds. Yellow shirts might handle 32 aircraft on deck at a time.

PURPLE SHIRTS

Fuel **technicians**, in purple shirts, handle all fuel on the carrier. Aircraft depend on fuel technicians to keep them moving. So do forklifts and dollies (wheeled platforms used to move objects). Fuel technicians might handle up to 200,000 gallons (757,000 l) of fuel on the carrier in just 1 day. Below deck, they check fuel quality carefully. A single spark could cause a huge explosion.

During **combat**, purple shirts refuel aircraft in the middle of the action. Sometimes they have to "hot pump," which means they move fuel to a plane or jet with live missiles, whirling blades, and aircraft landing all around.

THE AIR BOSS

An air officer, nicknamed the "air boss," directs flight deck activities and aircraft as far as 5 miles (8 km) away. This officer and the air officer assistant use computers to track movement and also oversee the deck from the windows of the island.

Because of their purple shirts, fuel technicians are sometimes called "grapes."

23

RED SHIRTS

Not every sailor is cut out for the dangerous job of a munitions expert. Munitions are weapons and ammunition. Munitions experts work below deck to put bombs and missiles together. Then they carefully move them through the carrier up to the flight deck. They take special routes and elevators far from the rest of the crew in case one of the missiles or bombs accidentally detonates, or explodes.

On deck, munitions experts load the munitions onto the jets. Their bright red shirts are easy to spot and alert other crewmembers that they're carrying weapons.

Red shirts load a bomb onto the wing of a jet.

TRICKY NIXIES

Besides having plenty of weapons and armed aircraft on board, aircraft carriers have other ways of protecting themselves in times of war. In the event of a submarine attack, a carrier can launch noise-making **decoy** targets called "Nixies." They drag behind the ship to attract torpedoes.

THE CONREP TEAM

Sailors who move fuel and other goods from a supply ship to the carrier are part of the connected replenishment, or ConRep, team. Replenishment simply means refueling or restocking, but this, too, can be dangerous on an aircraft carrier. Millions of gallons of flammable fuel are transported from ship to carrier through hoses.

Two pairs of sailors are needed for ConRep. Helmsmen steer the carrier, which has to sail in line next to the fuel ship. **Boatswain**'s mates work on the deck to move supply crates. Besides the danger of fuel fire, a snapping cable could slice a sailor in half!

The carrier may have to sail within 160 feet (49 m) of the supply ship for several hours. It's like steering two skyscrapers next to each other.

THE FLYING SQUAD

Fuel, nuclear reactors, and many onboard weapons make a carrier fire a real danger. The damage controlmen, or "flying squad," are there to fight fires. These sailors have to be ready 24 hours a day. They may also help with flooding and dangerous chemical spills.

SEARCH-AND-RESCUE CREW

Though it doesn't happen often, sometimes aircraft crash or land in the water. When this happens, search-and-rescue swimmers spring into action. After only a couple of minutes, they have their gear ready and take off in a rescue helicopter. They're lowered down on cables or jump right from the helicopter into the waters. Then they're pulled back into the helicopter along with the rescued crewmembers.

Day or night, warm or freezing waters, search-and-rescue teams are focused on saving lives. They—like all crew on an aircraft carrier—perform their extreme jobs the best they can for their country.

VULTURE'S ROW

Visitors on an aircraft carrier can get a bird's-eye view of the flight deck action from the top of the island on "vulture's row." This platform offers a great place to watch planes taking off and landing on the deck and a great view of the brave men and women on a carrier performing their jobs.

Whether a sailor falls overboard or a plane crashes into the water, the search-and-rescue team jumps into action whenever someone in the water needs to be saved.

GLOSSARY

accelerate: to increase in speed

ammunition: bullets, shells, and other things fired by weapons

boatswain: an officer on a ship in charge of the maintenance of the vessel and other equipment

combat: armed fighting between opposing forces

decoy: something used to trick someone or redirect their attention

knot: a unit of measurement for the speed at which a ship or aircraft travels

missile: a rocket used to strike something at a distance

nuclear reactor: a power plant that uses tiny pieces of matter called atoms to make energy

propulsion: the process by which an object such as a car, ship, or aircraft is moved forward

technician: a person who has special training in using equipment

weapon: something used to fight an enemy

FOR MORE INFORMATION

Books

Hamilton, John. *Aircraft Carriers*. Minneapolis, MN: ABDO Publishing, 2012.

Tillman, Barrett. Enterprise: *America's Fightingest Ship and the Men Who Helped Win World War II*. New York, NY: Simon & Schuster, 2012.

Zobel, Derek. *Nimitz Aircraft Carriers*. Minneapolis, MN: Bellwether Media, 2009.

Websites

Aircraft Carriers
www.pbs.org/wnet/warship/carriers/
Ask an expert questions, check out a photo slideshow, play games, and read an interview with an aircraft carrier captain.

Intrepid Sea, Air & Space Museum
www.intrepidmuseum.org
Learn all about one of the most famous aircraft carriers, the *Intrepid*, and other historical events and machines.

Toughest Carrier Jobs
military.discovery.com/tv/carrier-jobs/carrier-jobs.html
Read about the most extreme jobs on a carrier, with photos, quizzes, and puzzles.

INDEX